T0337291

In 650 days' time, our parents, the
retire. They'll stop feeding money into the system with taxes, and
start sucking it out with benefits. Why is it such a big problem?
Because there are so many of them and we don't have the
money to pay for them. Right now, in Britain, there are four
working people to support every pensioner. By the time all the
Boomers retire it'll be two to one. We are going to become
slaves to our parents, working longer hours, paying more taxes
and getting further into debt, just to pay for their retirement. This
is just a bit unfair, when you consider that Baby Boomers are the
richest generation that ever lived.

DO YOUR PARENTS LOVE YOU? OF COURSE THEY DO. BUT IT HASN'T STOPPED THEM ROBBING YOU BLIND

They might have given you the best start in life that they could. But they stopped short of providing for your future, or the future of your own children. They knew this problem was around the corner, and they had plenty of time and money to sort it out. But they chose not to. In fact, they chose to spend more money and use up greater resources than they had, knowing full well that the problem would be left for us – their own children – to sort out.

It's not just pensions. Look at all the material wealth that your parents have accumulated – the houses, the cars, the holidays, the savings. Did you expect to have the same things as them when you were growing up? Unless you're a hedge fund manager in the City, you can kiss those dreams goodbye. It's us who'll be paying off their billions of pounds' worth of Credit Crunch debt. And what about the environment? We've been left with the bill for clearing that up too.

GENERATION DEBT

Every new generation is defined by the icons and events of its time. For Generation X, it was supposed to be Grunge; MTV and the Internet for Generations Y and Z. All that went the way of Woolworths on the day the Boomers took control. Forget about iPlayer or YouTube, the symbol for generations born after 1964 is the credit card, because each and every one of us is sitting on a mountain of debt, built up and handed down to us by our folks.

You don't need to read this book to know how tough it is to live a normal life these days. You are living with the reality every day. Everything is expensive and in short supply. Nothing comes easy. And it's going to get worse. This manifesto will tell you what you can do about it.

Every baby in the UK is now born owing
£22,500

– his or her share of the £1.4 trillion Credit Crunch bailout. Added to which the average student graduates owing more than £20,000. Add all this together, and you're left with a generation owing more than £40,000 before they've earned their first pay packet. That's if you can get a job; there are 2.5 million people unemployed in the UK. One million of them are under 25 http://bit.ly/under25.

Pay packets, when you do finally find work, don't stretch beyond the absolute basics. First-time buyers need to earn an above-average salary to afford an ex-council flat, and you need a partner earning a full-time wage just to cover the food and heating. It's getting to the point where having children is a luxury.

Student debt is sold to us as an investment for our future, but that BA (Hons) certificate isn't worth the paper it's printed on. The more companies streamline and outsource their manpower, the less chance we have of winning well-paid, long-term contracts. Forget about jobs for life, university graduates are settling for part-time shop work or volunteering abroad.

These days, it's not unusual for 30-year-old professionals to go begging cap in hand to the Bank of Mum and Dad for bailouts, http://bit.ly/bankofmumanddad. And branches of the Hotel of Mum and Dad are springing up all the time – providing beds for a generation that studies hard for grades and toils diligently at work but still can't afford to make their own way.

And where are the proprietors of Mum and Dad Plc, now that the Credit Crunch has killed the party? They're safely tucked away in gated communities, or on permanent vacation in their places in the sun www.aplaceinthesun.com, leaving us to fight over the expensive dregs. If we have one certainty in the future, it's that we'll be working long past retirement age – which incidentally is being raised – to pay off the debts.

Heaven help the kids who are being born into this mess.

Go to http://bit.ly/debtoverseas to see how the exact same problem is kicking off overseas.

It was a different story when our parents were growing up. In fact, their lives sound like fairytales compared to ours. *They* fully expected to live a better life than their own folks. *They* drew decent wages from long-term jobs and received generous benefits from the welfare state. For them education was free and houses (not flats) were cheap and readily available. When prices boomed in the Eighties, they paid off their mortgages overnight. Suddenly flush with new money, rather than saving it sensibly, even working-class families were out buying new cars and colour TVs and taking holidays abroad. Mothers returned to work not just to cover the bills, but to improve the living standards of the family.

BLAME YOUR PARENTS

Those halcyon days are well and truly gone. We've been lumbered with so much debt and the cost of life's basics has shot up so high that we're guaranteed never to live as easily again. And it hasn't happened by accident. The awful truth is that, as our parents have climbed the ladder of social mobility, they have kicked the rungs from beneath them and prevented us from following them.

But don't take my word for it, just ask yourself this: who brought an end to the free education that they enjoyed when they were young? Who voted for low taxes while drawing easy handouts from the state? Who bought cheap houses, sold them for a fortune and priced out first-time buyers? Who awarded themselves record salaries and shipped the rest of the work overseas? Who cashed in on the market boom, then expected the taxpayer to bail them out when it went bust? You know who.

The enormous financial debt we've been handed is from their overspending. Everything about today's self-obsessed modern culture (record rates of divorce, suicide and drug addiction) comes from their megalomania. And the environmental crisis, dangerously close to the point of no return, is a hangover from their overconsumption. None of this is news to our parents though. The alarm bells have been ringing for decades, but they're world leaders at burying their heads in the sand.

Greedy? Selfish? Mummy and Daddy? It can't possibly be true? Here is what well-respected thinkers from across the political spectrum have to say:

'TWENTYSOMETHINGS WILL BE LUMBERED WITH HIGHER LEVELS OF TAXATION IN THE FUTURE TO PAY FOR THE LONGER AND BETTER RETIREMENTS OF THE AGEING BABY-BOOMER GENERATION ...

THAT'S NOT FAIR,'

SAYS RYAN SHORTHOUSE OF *THE GUARDIAN*.

'With their children departed and the mortgage paid off, their spending power is greater than that of any other age group,' says Melanie Phillips in the *Daily Mail*. 'They use it to pump up their lips and suck out their thighs, go trekking in Peru, and work out in the gym, eat organic food and irrigate their colons to cheat death and anticipate several more decades of looking after Me.'

'They won't be around to see the results,' says George Monbiot in *The Guardian*, '... they were brought up in a period of technological optimism; they feel entitled, having worked all their lives, to fly or cruise to wherever they wish.'

'For too long the world has been run by ... a generation that was simply born lucky,' says Sarah Vine in *The Times* (who is married to 43-year-old Shadow Secretary of State for Children, Schools and Families, Michael Gove). 'Now the party's over, they're not rolling up their sleeves either. Oh no, they're outta here, baby ... It's left to us to clear up.'

'The boomers have poisoned the wells and ploughed salt into the fields,' warns Bryan Appleyard in *The Sunday Times*. 'In the midst of their success and greed, the boomers forgot ... that society is a contract with three interested parties: the dead, the living and the unborn. Their children are paying the price of their amnesia. For the moment, they seem resigned, but, soon enough, they'll want their world back.'

THAT TIME IS NOW

Every generation has to struggle for something that it believes in – democracy, equal rights – but ours is nothing to do with race or class. It's going to be a fight between a debt-ridden minority of young adults and a glut of needy pensioners, who squandered the money they should have saved to support themselves and who will be supported by the working young.

Luckily, they have presented us with one big opportunity to make a change before the time bomb goes off.

CALL TO ACTION

There isn't much that we can do to fix the car crashes that our parents made in the past; it's a patch-up job at best. But we can prevent them from making any more in the future. The government has called a general election for 6 May this year. This is our one big opportunity to kick the Baby Boomers out of power before the future gets any worse.

The plan is very simple:
VOTE FOR CANDIDATES UNDER THE AGE OF 46 OR 65 AND OVER.

To find out who's standing in your local area, how old they are and what they stand for, visit **www.itsalltheirfault.com.**

We've never been very good at turning up to the election box. After all, what's the point of voting for people who lie as a matter of routine and break almost every election pledge that they make? And thanks to the expenses scandal, we know that they've been fiddling money out of the system for years. You'd be forgiven for thinking that politicians are all in it for themselves, and you'd be right; after all 70 per cent of MPs currently sitting in Parliament are Boomers. But that's okay; we won't be voting for them in any case.

There are plenty of alternatives standing in the general election. The following non-Boomer candidates could be a taste of things to come, if we get our act together and vote:

SAFE AS HOUSES
Sarah Teather, 35, MP For Brent East
http://bit.ly/SarahTeather

The youngest front-bencher in Parliament, Sarah was named one of the saints of the MPs' expenses scandal. She was eligible to claim tens of thousands of pounds in expenses, but chose not to. As the Shadow Housing Minister, she wants to bring the housing market back down to earth. 'For many, the dream of owning your own home is as far away as ever … Across the country 800,000 properties lie empty … Why can't some of these empty state-owned homes be offered cheaply to first-time buyers who are willing to put in the work to bring them up to scratch?'

YOUTH PIONEER
Rushanara Ali, 35. Standing in Bethnal Green & Bow
www.rushanaraali.org

Dubbed one of the most powerful Muslim women in the UK, Rushanara Ali is fighting for a seat in Parliament on the youth vote. 'The boards of ... public institutions that control billions of pounds of public money are ... dominated by middle-class, middle-aged white men. It is little wonder that many people, especially the young, feel disconnected from those that hold power and make decisions that affect their lives.' She's pledged to bring 19- to 25-year-olds into politics. 'The time is ripe,' she says, 'to help them take up positions of power.'

X VOICE OF REASON
Vince Cable, 67, MP for Twickenham
www.vincentcable.org.uk

In a parallel universe, Vince Cable is Prime Minister and a new world order is engulfing the idiocracy. He frequently warned that the economy was overdependent on cheap personal debt and an overvalued pound, long before the Credit Crunch kicked off. When the banks collapsed, he pushed for them to be nationalized rather than bailed out. And when the greedy RBS board threatened to walk over their £1.5 billion bonuses, Vince called their bluff and urged them to go. And he emerged as the cleanest senior MP in the expenses scandal.

X FEE SCRAPPER
Greg Mulholland, 39, MP for Leeds North West
www.gregmulholland.org

He campaigns to scrap student tuition fees. He fights against the sell-off and development of green belt land. He lobbies for the reinstatement of NHS dentists. And he's marched against the war in Iraq. If there's a reason why he's not more famous, it's because he's too busy doing his job to organize any PR.

X

SELF-LOATHING BOOMER
David Willetts, 54, MP for Havant
www.davidwilletts.co.uk

If there's one single Boomer worth voting for, it's Willetts who, on the basis of his speeches, could have written this book himself. 'If our political, economic and cultural leaders do not begin to discharge their obligations to the future, the young people of today will be taxed more, work longer hours for less money, have lower social mobility and live in a degraded environment in order to pay for their parents' quality of life.' Amen to that.

This isn't a fight between Left and Right or Labour versus Conservatives; it's between Generation Debt and the Baby Boomers AND IT'S A FIGHT WE'VE GOT TO WIN

Consider this book a manifesto and a call to action; a chance for those born in the Seventies and Eighties to respond to the chaos caused by those born in the Forties and Fifties. We are the generation that has to clear up their mess. This manifesto will explain why, and more importantly how.

AGE IS MORE THAN A NUMBER

Is it fair to say that every member of a generation behaves in the exact same way? **No**. Is it fair to say that a generation of people share certain characteristics? **Yes.** Each generation has a collective personality, which is shaped by the events of the time. For us, 9/11, the Credit Crunch and global warming defines who we are. For the Baby Boomers it was the post-war boom, which brought an explosion in population, unparalleled economic growth and a sea change in the way children were brought up.

Boomers are easy to identify. As of their birthday in 2010, they'll be aged between 46 & 64.

BOOMING POPULATION

The demographic model of the UK population looks like the side profile of your average middle-aged man: skinny chest and legs, and a great big sagging belly and arse in the middle. The skinny upper torso is the 'Silent Generation', in other words our grandparents, who were born before 1946. The skinny legs at the bottom are Generation Debt, born after 1964. The great big muffin top in the middle is the Baby Boomer generation, a population explosion that followed the Second World War.

The outbreak of peace in 1945 brought a tidal wave of euphoria to our grandparents, millions of whom returned home from the war to start new families. In the early Fifties, the majority of young suburban wives fell pregnant, which resulted in a sharp rise in births during the post-war years – the Baby Boom. By the end of the Boom in 1964, a whopping 11 million babies had been born.

You might think that we could have benefited equally, but with the advent of the Pill, birth control was so cheap, easy and effective that millions of Boomers put off having children until much later. This explains why our generation is so small in comparison.

BOOMING OPPORTUNITY

Boomer children were born into a golden era of opportunity. Britain was passing from an era of austerity in the Fifties (rations on food and energy, low employment) to an age of affluence and security in the Sixties, as the government pumped millions of pounds into rebuilding the country's infrastructure. Many industries had been nationalized in the late Forties and early Fifties, bringing the Bank of England, the telephone network, the airports, coal, gas, electricity, steel and transport into public ownership.

The new welfare state created in the late Forties brought an incredible sense of security to the country, promising to cover life's risks 'from the cradle to the grave'. The government built new schools and hospitals, provided rent-controlled housing, and handed out free education, free healthcare, unemployment benefit, sickness allowances, and pensions that you could actually live off.

In this public information film from 1948, Charley questions the need while the commentator explains how everyone in the UK will be protected from want, http://bit.ly/1948film.

With social security ticked off the to-do list, our parents set about raising the material standards of life. The international economy boomed, and Britain reached near full employment. Most of the jobs were for life. With so much opportunity Boomer teenagers grew up knowing that their prospects were better than their parents' had ever been. Truly, the British population had never had it so good.

New household goods flooded the market, catering for every possible need, and the old utilitarian products of the post-war period gave way to a bewildering array of cheap, attractive plastic goods, most of which came from the United States, the promised land of consumerism.

The trend for previous generations was to save for new purchases, making do and mending old things before they splashed out on something new. But with cheap credit and a bewildering array of choice, the young Boomers threw the old values of thrift and saving out of the window.

During the Sixties, consumer spending on household goods rose by 86% and on motor cars and motor cycles by 333%

The accessibility to desirable goods became so ubiquitous that Rab Butler, the Home Secretary in the early Sixties, boasted that 'People are divided not so much between "haves" and "have-nots" as between "haves" and "have-mores".'

Shopping was cheap but love was free. The sexual revolution allowed women to openly express themselves sexually for the first time, gays and lesbians started fighting for and winning their own rights, and the old rules of cohabitation and sex before marriage came tumbling down. Teenage Boomers of the Sixties had the incredible chance of living their twenties after the Pill and before AIDS; they were the first and last generation able to enjoy unlimited sex without any payback.

Work, social security, shopping and sex – it was all handed to Boomers on a plate. They were richer, freer and more secure than their parents or any generation before them. And it lasted so long that they began to take all this for granted as a way of life.

BOOMING SENSE OF SELF

Amidst all the opportunities of the Sixties, Boomer children were brought up with a new sense of self, and it was largely down to one book, *The Common Sense Book of Baby and Child Care* by Dr Benjamin Spock.

Before Spock, most parents brought up their children with tough love; babies were fed and put to sleep on a rigid schedule, and parents avoided picking up, kissing or hugging them whenever they cried. Giving in to a crying baby, it was thought, would only teach them to cry more. On the whole, the logic ran, it was better not to spoil, because this would prevent babies from becoming strong and morally minded citizens in a harsh world. But *The Common Sense Book* changed all that.

ACCORDING TO THE DR SPOCK MODEL, SCOLDING AND CONDESCENDING WERE *OUT*, AND FLEXIBILITY AND AFFECTION WERE *IN*.

Children were individuals, argued Spock, and needed to be 'smiled at, talked to, played with, fondled gently and lovingly'. Affection, as opposed to discipline, so he said, would make for happier and more productive lives.

Spock's ideas resonated with parents of the Fifties and Sixties, who wanted to protect their children from the fear and deprivation that they suffered during the Second World War. The book sold over 50 million copies, outselling every other book except the Bible. Parents ditched the 'one size fits all' philosophy of child rearing and brought up their children less like citizens and more like individuals. Caught up in this new outpouring of affection, many parents took to pampering their baby's every need, although Spock himself advised against it. 'Parents who aren't afraid to be firm when it is necessary,' he said, 'can get good results with either moderate strictness or moderate permissiveness.'

Citizens are loyal to authority. Individuals tend to rebel against it. And so the Boomer teens – confident, affluent and healthy – began to rebel against the system that had treated them so well, rallying in the streets for peace and love. The Right Wing was duly up in arms, labelling Spock as 'The Father of Permissiveness'. Norman Vincent Peale, a powerful religious leader of the time, warned prophetically that the world was 'paying the price of two generations that followed the Dr Spock baby plan of instant gratification of needs'.

GENERATION ME

If there is one decade that defines the Boomers, it is, of course, the Sixties. The optimism, the individualism and the excess of the Sixties are burnt on the memory of our parents. These are the shared experiences that triggered common traits in the character of our parents. And they are one of the reasons why the music, art and fashion are rehashed and revisited with a punishing frequency.

SELFISH

Indulged, protected and privileged, Boomers are prone to Pampered Child Syndrome. Children who are loved, nurtured and protected 'too much', according to clinical psychologist Dr Maggie Mamen, grow up believing that 'they are entitled to the same rights as adults, but ... are not ready to accept grown-up responsibilities'. In the rush to provide their children with the opportunities they themselves never had, the parents of Baby Boomers forgot to 'strike an effective balance between caring for and nurturing children while at the same time maintaining authority and demanding respect'.

Boomers were raised by their parents to believe that they were special, and conditioned by their teachers to think as individuals. Being the wealthiest generation of all time, it's fair to say that they were special. But the endless opportunity and the constant drive to build their self-esteem went to their heads. Personal growth and self-help were more important to them than any sense of duty to the people around them.

The lyrics to Queen's worldwide Boomer hit say it all. http://bit.ly/Iwantitall

Previous generations, who lived through the Depression and the war, consumed sparsely and managed their expectations and aspirations. But to the Boomers, driven by a sense of entitlement, personal needs are more important and they expect them delivered on a platter. The oversized homes, the piles of possessions, the extravagant vacations:

BOOMERS WANT IT ALL

WHATEVER THE COST

There are hundreds of advertising manuals devoted to Boomers, but they all point to one character trait: the selfish individual. 'Boomers want special treatment,' according to *50 Things Every Marketer Needs to Know About Boomers Over 50*, 'and feel entitled to it. They want your special treatment because they think they deserve it, or have earned it.'

Twelve per cent of teenagers surveyed in the early Fifties agreed with the statement 'I am an important person'; by the late Eighties this had risen to 80 per cent. 'As commendable as it is for children to have high self-esteem,' says Lillian G. Katz, 'many of the practices advocated in pursuit of this goal may instead inadvertently develop narcissism in the form of excessive preoccupation with oneself.'

There is a point where a healthy sense of self-worth tips over into self-infatuation. To fully understand the Boomer market, *Advertising to Baby Boomers* advised that 'one must assume the mindset of a person who believes he is part of the single most important generation to walk the planet'.

Self-loving Boomer culture is all around us. Love yourself! Be your own best friend! These are the mantras of the self-help book market, which exploded soon after Boomers learnt to read. It was all summed up by Whitney Houston, in the Boomer nirvana that was the Eighties, with her best-selling anthem 'The Greatest Love of All'.

The greatest love, in case you hadn't already worked it out, IS THE LOVE FOR ONESELF

Fifty years of navel gazing has destroyed any lingering sense of collectivism in our country, where neighbours are strangers and relationships are part time. The reliance on friends and family for support has been reclassified as 'co-dependency'. If Boomers swapped their self-help manuals for a legitimate bit of psychology, they'd find that most specialists agree: human happiness relies more on stable relationships than self-love.

GREEDY

Compare the logos of CND and Mercedes Benz – they look almost exactly the same. In the Sixties, 'selling out' was an insult. Now it's an aspiration.

With so much emphasis on the self, Boomers were bound to focus on individual rights as their cause célèbre. As teenagers, they fought for political rights and sexual freedom. But the fight gradually morphed into the right for instant gratification. According to Carol Craig, at the Centre for Confidence and Well-being, this individualism came to represent not autonomy, but self-centredness and the satisfaction of personal wants. Individualism, Craig argues, has left Boomers 'pursuing constant gratification, with much of this disguised by a show of self-confidence'.

The quest for constant gratification has driven consumer growth ever since the Sixties. With high self-worth comes high expectations, and so the Boomers disposed with their parents' 'make do and mend' mantra in favour of 'buy now pay later'. Endless innovative luxuries, delivered to the door, were designed to be binned just as soon as the next fad hit the stores. The constant refitting of houses, the endless gadgets, the new wardrobes; Boomers have spent a fortune on novelty and junk.

Personal fulfilment, according to research http://bit.ly/Boomerresearch, is the number 1 priority for today's Boomers, and self-indulgence is the preferred means. In the evangelical churches of America, it has become a virtue. But one weekly visit to church wasn't enough; Boomers scrapped Sunday trading laws so that they could worship consumerism at their shiny new, cathedral-like shopping malls. Next time you visit your parents, take a look at the enormous piles of stuff they have bought, and now hoard, in the loft. It's no wonder that self-storage is one of the fastest growing industries in the UK.

IRRESPONSIBLE

There is a rule of thumb in advertising which says you should communicate with consumers as though they are more sophisticated than they really are. The core market for *Just 17* magazine, for example, used to be 13-year-old girls who were desperate to act older than their age. Boomers are the exception to this rule. 'Boomers at 50 see themselves some 12 years younger than they really are,' according to one report at http://bit.ly/BabyBoomer, 'that means they don't associate themselves with any imagery connected to being old.'

The phenomenon even has a name: Middlescence, the turbulent, rebellious middle age of the Baby Boomer generation. In other words it is adolescence a second time around. 'Boomers may never mature,' says the Boomer Project, an advertising agency dedicated to harnessing the grey pound; '… they reject any and all age-related labels to describe themselves.' Forty years ago, our parents chanted The Who's immortal line 'Hope I die before I get old.' In the end, they chose to postpone the inevitable by regressing to their youth. No wonder the anti-ageing business is doing so well. Terrified of maturity, they flock to spas for miracle treatments, and guzzle food supplements laced with magical elixirs for long life. According to a recent survey, at http://bit.ly/Boomersurvey,

2/3 of Boomers want to change their looks with cosmetic surgery and one in ten has already gone under the knife

Middlescent Boomers, according to the think tank Demos, are 'refusing to be constrained by expectations of "appropriate behaviour"'. That would be fine, if inappropriate behaviour was limited to dinner party spliffs and Rolling Stones concerts. Unfortunately, it is a great deal more harmful than that. If we can cite one good reason why our futures have been mortgaged to the hilt by our parents, it is because they cannot and will not live up to their responsibilities like adults.

It's all worryingly similar to Peter Pan Syndrome. They want all the trappings of adulthood, but they shy away from the responsibility and the sacrifice that comes with it. Like Peter Pan, they break conventions to serve their own purposes, with little regard for the feelings and rights of others, and they justify it all with a sense of righteous entitlement.

HYPOCRITICAL

With a casual attitude to responsibility, and an unassailable belief in their self-worth, Boomers bounce between opposing values with ease. They revolted against 'the man' when they were young, but were happy to join him when the price was right. Free love, non-violence, equal opportunity, no 'sell out' turned into fads when these principles required any kind of personal sacrifice. They rebelled against the Puritanism of their parents, then did an about turn and ended up lurching to the Right; after all, they were forced to knuckle down and make some cash if they wanted to tick off all the cars and second homes on their shopping lists.

They drank, they smoked, they shagged around & they broke the rules

Nowadays you can't even put your rubbish out without risking a fine. They frown on single parent families, call the unemployed 'scroungers' and demand ever-tougher action against drink and drugs.

'We need to mend our broken society!' shout the Conservatives. 'Marriage is important!' they say, offering young families a £100 bribe to stay together.

NO PRIZES FOR GUESSING WHICH GENERATION'S DIVORCE RATE SHOT UP BY

700%

IN THEIR LIFETIME

Hypocrisy is the unconscious act of self-deception, a way of rationalizing the uncomfortable facts of life which, in the case of our parents, is a complete volte-face of the principles that they define themselves by.

Sex, drugs and rock and roll – they invented all that. Not us. But they love to bash us over the head with high-minded values, flicking through the *Daily Mail* with one hand, loading a Bob Dylan CD with the other. 'They professed to go with the flow,' quips commentator Joe Queenan, 'but it was actually the cash flow.'

BOOMERS AT LARGE

The first wave of Boomers left school to start work in the mid-Sixties. They were still rising through the ranks in the Seventies and early Eighties, making waves as consumers and young parents. It's only in the last twenty years that they have started to take control, replacing their own parents in business, politics and the media. In 2010, as chance would have it, Boomers are at the peak of their influence. They are the establishment and the mainstream. Events on the local, national and international stage are played out between them. And the culture we find ourselves living in today is almost entirely down to them.

MASTERS OF THE UNIVERSE: BOOMER BUSINESSMEN

In 1996 the average salary of a FTSE 100 CEO was thirty-six times greater than the average salary in their company. Ten years later, this gap has widened to more than a hundred times.

Business is business; it always has been, and always will be, cutthroat. But just like old-fashioned street fighting (no knives, guns or dirty tricks), the rules of gentlemanly throat cutting have become more ruthless since Boomers took their seats in the boardroom. Best business practice can now be summarized as follows:

1. **Kill off / take over the competition**
2. **Lay off staff**
3. **Create regulation to cover your tracks**
4. **Build a business in which a select few get the gold mine and most people get the shaft**

The Credit Crunch, and the world economic downturn that followed, is the product of reckless disregard for the rules, insatiable greed and a rollicking sense of self-regard, all characteristics that have become institutionalized in the Boomer business world. It's no coincidence that the high-flying businessmen from the Pampered Child era refer to themselves as Masters of the Universe.

They mis-sold pensions and mortgages to a public that didn't know any better. They ruthlessly cut costs, outsourced jobs, stripped assets and worked for short-term payoffs. And they achieved all this by pushing for financial deregulation – gradually tearing up the age-old financial rulebook that was written to stop this sort of thing happening in the first place.

Of course, there have been financial crises and corporate losses in the past. But all of the record-breaking disasters have unfolded with Boomers at the helm. All the big financial heads that rolled during the Credit Crunch, from Stan O'Neal (56) at Merrill Lynch to Northern Rock's Adam Applegarth (45), were Boomers.

The largest corporate loss in history, $61.7 billion by insurance company AIG, was overseen by Martin Sullivan, aged 55. The American taxpayer bailed out the company to the tune of $182.5 billion. Sullivan received $25.4 million for his trouble.

The largest corporate bankruptcy of all time was posted by Lehman Brothers for $3.9 billion under the stewardship of Richard Fuld, 64. Lehman was one of the world's oldest and most respected investment banks until, under Fuld, it plunged headlong into sub-prime mortgages. It was forced to sell off $6 billion in assets in 2008, and dragged the stock market, and employees, down with it. Richard Fuld, meanwhile, kept $480 million in pay and bonuses.

IT WILL COME AS NO SURPRISE THAT ALL THIRTEEN MEMBERS OF THE RBS BOARD, WHO RECENTLY THREATENED TO WALK IF THEIR £1.5 BILLION BONUSES WERE BLOCKED, ARE

BABY BOOMERS

Last year, General Motors posted an annual loss of $38.7 billion, the largest ever for a car company. Their CEO, Rick Wagoner, is 56. The biggest ever one-day fall in the London Stock Exchange was overseen by Mervyn King, the 61-year-old Governor of the Bank of England.

In 2009, *Time* magazine published a list of the twenty-five most blameworthy businessmen and financiers responsible for the current crash. Their average age is 61.

OUR VERY OWN SIR FRED GOODWIN, AGE 51, WAS VOTED AS THE GREEDIEST BANKER OF ALL TIME. NO WONDER, FOR HE WAS RESPONSIBLE FOR THE BIGGEST FINANCIAL LOSS IN THE HISTORY OF THE UK

Fred joined RBS in 1998 after a long and rewarding stint of free education at Paisley Grammar School and Glasgow University followed by work as an accountant. At RBS he soon earned his nickname of Fred the Shred, for cutting costs and jobs. Goodwin built the bank up with aggressive takeovers, and ruthlessly cut staff in order to generate bigger profits. In the same year that Goodwin axed 18,000 jobs from NatWest Bank, he bought a £17.5 million Dassault Falcon executive jet to fly himself around the world. He was knighted for services to the banking industry months later.

During his ten-year reign, RBS made over thirty thousand people redundant. With the money saved, they built new headquarters in Edinburgh for £350 million and headquarters in the USA for $500 million. They splashed out £200 million in celebrity endorsements. As the bank careered towards huge losses, Sir Fred redecorated his office with wallpaper costing £1,000 a roll. He spent £5.3 million lavishly refurbishing a grade A listed building – dubbed 'Sir Fred's Pleasure Dome' by staff – that was barely used. He paid out £100,000 a month on part-time chauffeurs and flew fruit in daily from Paris. Fred the Shred's reckless Boomer greed finally ended in disaster when the £49 billion takeover of ABN Amro, Europe's biggest ever banking takeover, stretched funds too far. He left shareholders with the biggest loss in UK corporate history, and the taxpayer with a £33 billion bailout bill.

For his services, he paid himself a £16 million pension, drawing £703,000 a year for life.

His self-regard and greed knowing no bounds, he ignored pressure from his shareholders, the media, Parliament and even the Prime Minister to hand back the retirement package. In the end, the universe finally crashed around Master Fred's ears and, retreating to a gated private estate on the Riviera, he shredded his own pension to £200,000 per year.

DOUBLE STANDARDS: BOOMERS IN POLITICS

From the moment our parents took junior positions in politics, in the late Eighties and early Nineties, they have diluted and in many cases dissolved most of the privileges that they benefited from when they were our age, one by one. In the last twenty years, the government has sold off our phone lines, TV stations, gas, airports, airways, steel, water, electricity, and they pocketed £50 billion (at today's prices) in the process. The little that's left – education, healthcare, housing, pensions – is either underfunded, prohibitively expensive or both. Every time our parents were given the option of maintaining services with taxes, or keeping the money for themselves, the majority of them voted for cash; and the politicians duly obliged.

Westminster is dominated by Boomers. The average age of MPs in the UK is 50.1 years and there is not one who paid tuition fees when they were growing up. We all do now.

From 1989 to 1997, the Conservatives ran our schools and universities into the ground with a 36 per cent reduction in funding for every full-time student. Then Labour swept into Parliament, screaming 'Education, Education, Education'. What they meant to say was 'Fees, Fees, Fees' as they set about ending free higher education for ever.

Every single Education Secretary since 1998 educated

themselves at university for free (except Alan Johnson who didn't go). And every single one of them has voted strongly in favour of making us pay. Each and every one of them is a Boomer.

David Blunkett, 49, was educated for free at a college for the blind, originally established by a Victorian philanthropist and an anti-slavery campaigner, followed eventually by Sheffield University. But Blunkett enslaved future generations to debt, by moving to abolishing free higher education. He went on to abolish student maintenance grants in 1998.

Charles Clarke, educated for free at Oxford in the Seventies, went a step further by introducing £3,000 annual top up fees, despite a Labour manifesto commitment not to do so.

Fifty-seven-year-old Lord Mandelson, whose department now looks after education, is pushing for an increase in fees to £7,000. Students, says Mandelson, 'have to face up to the challenge of paying for excellence'. A former member of the Young Communist League, Lord Mandelson enjoyed an excellent education at Oxford. For free.

If there's no obvious difference between the main parties today it's because they are all working to the same agenda: their own. The Boomer mindset is stuck on 'me', and politicians simply cannot help but act in their own self-interest; to the extent that they'll pull back the rights and privileges of others to protect their own. This is the generation that marched in the streets for freedom, but ended up lining them with CCTV cameras. Boomer politicians from the Right and the Left have gradually abandoned their principles and migrated to the centre – the self-centre.

If ever there was an archetypal Boomer politician, it would be the former Blair Babe, 53-year-old Hazel Blears. All leathered-up on her Yamaha motorbike, she is one of the worst offenders. Caught red-handed fiddling her sizeable expenses, she is prone to Boomer greed. But it's the hypocrisy of it all that makes her first among equals in the Boomer political class.

Blears voted strongly in favour of university top-up fees, having enjoyed a long and productive education for free. As a rising young star of the Labour Party, she vigorously opposed the abolition of Clause IV – Labour's once untouchable commitment to nationalization – but helped to privatize large chunks of health, education and transport with Private Finance Initiatives.

She voted for stronger regulation of the tax system, but was later investigated for fiddling capital gains tax to the tune of £13,000. She voted against minimum wage rights for part-time workers, but claimed the maximum allowable expenses, down to the last penny, on her three homes. And let's not forget that Hazel Blears' shtick is that she's a salt of the earth girl from Salford.

IN 2008, ONE-THIRD OF SALFORD'S CHILDREN WERE LIVING IN POVERTY. MEANWHILE, HAZEL BLEARS WAS LIVING IN THE ZETTER HOTEL IN LONDON

one of the '50 coolest hotels in the world' according to *Condé Nast Traveller.*

GRUMPY OLD MEN – CELEBRITY BOOMERS

Endless opportunity. Relative security. Easy money. On paper, Baby Boomers should be the happiest, most optimistic people on Earth. But the teen rebels have become professional moaners, complaining about new fads that make them feel old, or bemoaning new laws that stop them doing whatever they want.

A few years ago, Boomers found the perfect outlet for this frustration in the TV show *Grumpy Old Men* (and later *Grumpy Old Women*). This was the chance for wealthy ageing Boomers like Rick Wakeman and Jilly Cooper, and others such as Rick Stein, A.A. Gill and, of course, Jeremy Clarkson, to moan about how awful life is, while at the same time being the most prosperous generation of all time and living in a country that gave them so much.

'Is this the world we created?' they whine to snatches of 'Those Were the Days'. Watched over by the state, homogenized by business, intimidated by teenagers, imprisoned in their gated homes. Is this the world they created? The answer, of course, is yes.

You don't need a degree in psychology to work out what triggers the Boomer grumps. It's all down to their sense of entitlement, the belief that they deserve whatever, whenever they want. It doesn't matter how much wealth or freedom they've got, they still want more. And when something stops them from enjoying it, they tend to throw their toys out of the pram, complaining to the *Daily Mail* about the (mostly imaginary) killjoys that are out to spoil their fun.

WHY CAN'T THEY BUILD ANOTHER EXTENSION ON THEIR HOUSE? WHY CAN'T THEY TAKE FIVE HOLIDAYS A YEAR BY PLANE? IT'S THEIR RIGHT! THEY EARNED IT!*

* AND NO MEDDLING POLITICALLY CORRECT BUREAUCRAT IS GOING TO STOP THEM!

The conflict between teen rebel and grumpy old man produces a bewildering array of double standards. The generation famous for mini skirts, LSD and the Summer of Love demands that today's teenagers be strung up for being irresponsible drunken layabouts.

When they're not moaning, they're embarrassing themselves pretending to be teenagers. The balding accountant in the flash BMW; the jowly old rocker at the back of the Keane gig; the middle-aged mum in the shopping centre dolled up in the same gruesome Ugg boots and Juicy Couture tracksuit as her kids: all tragic evidence of the Peter Pan Syndrome in full bloom. It would all be a harmless spectacle if they weren't still in charge of culture. But they are.

Have you ever wondered why there's so little new music on the BBC, why it runs endless retrospectives on dinosaurs like Roxy Music and Led Zeppelin, why culture programmes look like they're made by your dad? It's because the man in charge of that stuff is 63-year-old Alan Yentob. 'I grew up listening to the Beatles, the blues and Jimi Hendrix,' says Alan, '... but we are all ghetto kids now.' So he jets off to personally interview Eminem. The toe-curling results have been deleted from YouTube to preserve the dignity of all involved.

When 50-year-old private equity guru Guy Hands took over EMI, he promised to save 'The Greatest Recording Organization in the World'. How did this startling new vision for twenty-first-century music take form? A Beatles anthology CD boxset of course! All the good bands have since left, leaving Boomer mummy's boy Robbie Williams to rescue the spreadsheet.

Madonna (51) and Bono (50) dominate the charts and the stadiums with grim inevitability. And without fail, Radio 1 gives them heavy promotion. Why does the nation's 'popular music station for

15–29-year olds' sound like a hernia hospital radio station?
Because it's run by Andy Parfitt, a 50-year-old Baby Boomer.

FAST CARS?
DAD ROCK?
SAGGING WAISTLINE?
Without a doubt, Jeremy Clarkson – perpetual adolescent and serial whinger – was born to be the poster boy of his generation.

His screw-you attitude resonates with Boomer males who absolutely refuse to take responsibility for anyone other than themselves. In 2008, 50,000 Boomers signed a petition on the Number 10 website to 'Make Jeremy Clarkson Prime Minister'. Could so many people really be that stupid? The awful truth is here http://bit.ly/clarksonforpm.

And then there are the jeans; the terrible loose-fit Levi's belted over the paunch. His generation stole jeans from youth culture, and they'll never give them back. Ever since Dress Down Friday (their hideous invention), jeans have become pretty much unreturnable in any case. Clarkson played a pivotal role in this theft. Fashion experts attribute Levi's mid-Nineties sales crash to the 'Clarkson Effect' as a legion of dads attempted to dress like their kids. Sales of Levi's have never fully recovered since.

More calamitous to our future, however, is the irresponsible behaviour dressed up in lad humour. On *Top Gear*, the ultimate

Boomer behaving badly show, Clarkson scored points with middle-aged children when he drove a 4X4 across areas of outstanding natural beauty and scientific interest to reach the North Pole. It might have looked like a laugh, but it was really a two-fingered salute to the 'killjoy' environmentalists in the name of hard-won personal freedom. 'I do have a disregard for the environment ...' he said later, 'I think the world can look after itself and we should enjoy it as best we can.' And so we return to this sense of entitlement – the in-built belief that self-fulfilment is a God-given right, regardless of the cost.

The mind of the middle-aged rebel is a confusing thing. The environmental movement, says Clarkson, is run by 'old trade unionists and CND lesbians' – the very same radicals that propped up the state, gave peace a chance and defined the generation he so reveres. The Greens, the Reds, the Nannies and the Bureaucrats have turned the world mad, he whinges, but what can Boomers do to make it sane again? The answer is simple: jump in a gas-guzzler and tear down the road singing 'I Feel Free' by Cream.

THEM AND US

Three grand overdrafts? Multiple credit cards? One hundred and twenty-five per cent mortgages? Debt is so commonplace nowadays that it's joined death and taxes as certainties in life.

There's even an iPhone application that arranges short-term pay day loans, because wages never seem to cover the bills. Be under no illusion, there was a life before debt. These, today, are the cold hard facts that our generation will have to deal with:

THE MONEY

THEM – £500 Billion in the Black

Baby Boomers are by far the wealthiest and most powerful generation in Britain to have ever lived. They own nearly £500 billion in assets, which is four-fifths of the entire nation's wealth. They are the nation's landlords, owning and occupying more houses than anyone else. They have the highest average income and expenditure in the population. And they are about to become even wealthier, as they inherit the houses and savings of their own parents, who were thrifty enough to leave any kind of legacy. Boomers now hold so much capital that parents are loaning money out like banks. Last year, the Bank of Mum Dad loaned an average of £12,000 to one in two children.

US – £2.2 Trillion in the Red

In 1970, when many of our parents were graduating and buying their first homes, the average person owed 60 per cent of their annual income in debt. In 2010, young people owe 173 per cent. For most of us, mortgages and pensions are out of the question; we are getting into debt just trying to keep up with the basics.

On average, we owe £9,016 in personal debts

(excluding mortgages). And let's not forget the national debt that we'll be paying off for the rest of our lives. We, as taxpayers, currently owe £2.2 trillion – the worst level since the 1950s, when Britain was paying back its war debts. For ours, and future generations, there is no escape. Every child in the UK is now born with £22,500 debt as a result of the Credit Crunch bailout. By the time those babies graduate, they'll each start their working lives owing over £40,000 in personal and national debt and that's in today's money. At the last count, there were 1.5 million 18–24-year-olds in poverty in England and Wales. And let's not forget pensioners on the other side of the Baby Boom – one in three people over the age of 64 in the UK is currently living in poverty.

THE SCHOOLS

THEM

University life for Baby Boomers can be summed up with just one word: free. Not one student was charged for tuition. In fact, most students were *paid* to go. Local education authorities assessed how wealthy students' families were, and on that basis gave them a maintenance grant, which didn't have to be paid back. In the early Eighties, a student was given anything up to £4,000 in today's money. Students with exceptional abilities could apply for State Scholarships, which gave all or sometimes more than the full grant, regardless of how much their parents earned. It wasn't a luxury holiday, but they rarely graduated out of pocket.

US

University is so expensive that some female students are stripping and selling sex, just to pay the fees. This was the real life story behind the glitzy façade of *Belle de Jour*. Little wonder, when the average student in 2010 graduates with over £20,000 of debt. Tony Blair abolished free maintenance grants in 1998 and replaced them with Student Loans, which had to be paid back. With interest. Then, in 1999, local education authorities stopped paying tuition fees, and the cost was passed on to students. These fees have risen from the original £1,000 per year to £3,225. But it's going to get a lot worse; universities and Lord Mandelson are pushing the government to increase the fees to £7,000 or more.

On that basis, students will be clocking up close to
£30,000 in debts

which will take graduates an average of thirteen years at today's salaries of work to clear.

THE WELFARE STATE

THEM

Imagine a world where you were guaranteed an affordable house to rent, free healthcare and dentistry, and financial support when life took a turn for the worse. It used to exist. Rent control, full employment, universal healthcare: these were just a few of the benefits they drew from the welfare state, which was originally set up to eradicate the 'five great evils' of want, ignorance, disease, squalor and idleness. The downside was that it cost money, and adult Boomers consistently voted for low taxes while they earned high wages. Without enough money in the pot, the welfare state gradually started to be dismantled in the late – Eighties – the same time that Boomers began to enter government.

US

Spending on welfare as a proportion of the country's income has halved since its peak in 1994. It has become more and more difficult to apply for unemployment and housing benefit, child support, sickness benefit or a pension. And for the few that do qualify, they're worth a fraction of what used to be paid out. State pensions, which Boomers are about to enjoy, will probably disappear by the time we retire. All the money we paid into national insurance will have long been spent. The current government plans to offer people under the age of 30 the chance to opt out of the state pension system entirely.

Free eye tests were stopped in the Eighties, while prescription charges for drugs have rocketed, and it's ever more difficult to apply for free dental care. In 1990, 90 per cent of adults in the UK used NHS dentists. It has since dropped to less than 50 per cent of the population. Eleven million people get no dental care whatsoever. In 2009, more than 22,000 people had to be admitted to hospital for emergency dental treatment because they couldn't afford to pay for the work.

And it's going to get worse. NHS managers have warned that the National Health Service faces a budget shortfall so large that it cannot possibly survive without drastic cuts.

Ministers are currently considering making us pay to visit GPs.

Provision for legal aid is being reduced. Free bus passes for the young and old may end. The list goes on and on.

None of this really matters if you can afford to pay for private healthcare or a private pension or a mortgage on your own home. But the future for those that can't is looking very, very grim.

THE HOUSING

THEM

Eighty-five per cent of Baby Boomers in the UK own their homes. They were mostly bought on the cheap, and the majority of them were Des Res. House prices were relatively low in the Seventies, when our parents began buying homes, but it was Margaret Thatcher's Housing Act that unleashed the runaway property market that exists today. It was like a cut-price high street sale; council housing tenants who had rented for at least three years could buy their home for 33 per cent less than the market price; 44 per cent off for a flat. Best of all, if you'd been renting for twenty years, the discount was 50 per cent, all bankrolled by the taxpayer. One million six hundred thousand homes were sold off in England alone. House prices rose steadily, and our parents cashed in and traded up the property ladder with ease.

The average house price in 1970 was £4,974. In today's money, that's £60,235. Our parents would have had to borrow three times their annual income on a mortgage. In return, they got a two-bedroom house with a garden.

US

House prices in the UK have risen by thirty-one times since 1970. The average price is now £158,871. And you'll have to borrow 6.5 times your annual salary to pay it off.

In the last decade alone, house prices have risen by 90 per cent, raking in huge profits for ageing sellers, but pricing us out of the market. Ours is the last generation that can reasonably expect to buy our own homes. John Healy, the 50-year-old Conservative housing spokesman (with two homes) says so himself here: http://bit.ly/JohnHealy

Almost half of all mortgages taken out in the Eighties were with first-time buyers. In 2010, it has dropped to 15 per cent. Affordable housing is in such short supply that in the future people will have to wait until they inherit property when their parents die (unless it has not already been sold off).

Renting at the Hotel of Mum and Dad is fast becoming the only sensible option. One in five students now lives at home while they finish their degrees.

And one-third of 20–34-year-olds are moving back home – priced out of the market by their landlord parents.

For first-time buyers, there are now only two steps on to the housing ladder: take out a 125 per cent fifty-year mortgage on an ex-council house and work past retirement to pay it off, or rent a small flat and wait for your parents to die.

THE WORK

THEM

Baby Boomers were born into a sustained period of full employment. That's not to say that everyone worked, but anyone who wanted a job could have one. At one point, unemployment dropped to a record low of just 1 per cent. Unemployment benefit was easy to apply for; it was a safety net, which meant graduates didn't have to rush into the first job they found. Stop and consider this for a moment: that meant waiting for a job that you actually wanted to do!

Jobs were usually for life. Employers offered commitment and the employees repaid it with loyalty. It wasn't unusual for companies to throw anniversary parties for staff who had worked there for ten, twenty, even thirty years. And yes, the old wives' tales are true: you received a gold watch and a pension when you finally retired. In 1975, the average time spent working at a company was 10.4 years.

US

The average length of new jobs in 2010 is fifteen months. Jobs for life have turned into a life of jobs – if you can get them. Last year, 40,000 students left university and headed straight for the dole queue. And they were just the ones who could apply for support. The average number of graduates chasing every job has risen to 48 and starting salaries remain frozen.

Plus we work between 5 & 10 hours more per week than our parents did.

And we don't earn much more money, in real terms, to show for it.

Young Boomers regularly took paid apprenticeships as their first step into the job market. But we face a seemingly endless string of internships – essentially free labour with no promise of employment – before a company will pay us for our time.

Our country is the sixth richest in the world. It is significantly wealthier than it was thirty years ago. Why do we have to struggle with short-term contracts, temporary unemployment or multiple menial jobs? Because *they*, in their managerial positions, have outsourced or axed jobs so *they* can boost their portfolios of shares.

The official rate of unemployment in the UK is 7.8 per cent. But that figure is artificially low, because it has become so difficult to sign on. People who are out of work but aren't entitled to benefit have been reclassified as 'economically inactive'. At the last count, there were six times as many of them as on the dole.

Half the jobs lost over the past year were from our generation. The UK's young jobless rate is the highest in Europe. Right now, almost 1 million people under the age of 25 are out of work.

Here's a very depressing video that spells it out in full http://bit.ly/jobsvideo.

THE COST OF LIVING

Thirty years ago, money was not only easier to make, it had greater value. In 2010, a single person renting a small council flat needs to earn at least £13,400 a year to afford the minimum standard of living. That's more than double the cost in the Seventies.

	THEM (1970)	US (2010)
Weekly family food bill	£32.20	£91.61
Gallon of petrol	£1.65	£4.36
Pint of beer	59p	£3.02
Cinema ticket	£1.66	£7.02
Football season ticket	£64	£471.96
Loaf of white bread	38p	92p
Frozen chicken	57p	£3.27
20 cigarettes	£1.03	£6.46
Haircut	£24	£63
Pair of jeans	£20	£54

All prices adjusted for inflation

THE ENVIRONMENT

THEM

In the late Sixties, a book called *The Population Bomb* painted a chilling scenario of the world's fate if people, and their principal bi-product pollution, continued to rocket. Over 2 million Boomers bought the book, and a few years later, both Greenpeace and Friends of the Earth were born. Since then, they've talked endlessly about the environment, but done very little for it. Between 1980 and 2001, the world's electricity consumption rose by 88 per cent. World carbon dioxide emissions have grown by 36 per cent. Half of the earth's mature tropical forests that until 1947 covered the planet have now been cleared.

Boomers might claim to have started the Green movement, but all that their banner waving has achieved is a series of failed talks, empty promises and missed targets. And Boomers are all talk and no action: with their 'high disposable income and jet-set lifestyles', they have the highest carbon footprint in the UK compared to any other age group. Since the first UN Earth Summit of 1992, Boomers have delayed action on the environment by pushing deadlines ever further into the future – our future to be precise.

US

The environmental outlook that our generation faces is overwhelmingly grim. According to the *United Nations Global Environment Outlook*, many of the world's farming regions are at the limits of their production, three-quarters of the world's marine stocks have been fished beyond their limits and pollution is now a major cause of death and disease. Species extinction has accelerated to the extent that

36%
of all known species are now listed as endangered.

The world's population is now so big that we need more than a single planet's resources to sustain us. With much of the world's resources already spent, the leftovers cost a fortune. Oil production is expected to peak around 2013. Coal, at the current rate of consumption, won't last beyond 2067. And yet the International Energy Agency estimates that global energy consumption will double by 2050.

THEY BUY NOW. WE PAY LATER

The difference between Them and Us is clear. Theirs was the most prosperous and privileged generation of all time. And ours is one of the most indebted, facing a future of almost certain gloom.

The income gap between the middle-aged rich and young poor is now the widest since records began. Not since the Second World War has the government borrowed so much or our country been so heavily in debt.

MAKE NO MISTAKE, WE WILL BE WORKING PAST RETIREMENT AGE TO PAY IT OFF, WHILE THEY CRACK OPEN THEIR NEST EGGS AND KICK BACK ABROAD

It's happening already. The fastest growing holiday market in the UK is for Luxury Grey Cruises. Here they are, playing bridge, splashing in the pool and sipping cocktails aboard their vast floating pleasure domes, staffed by smartly dressed natives who are on hand to fulfil their every need. It all sounds rather lovely, http://bit.ly/luxuryvideo.

Seven out of ten people who will retire in the next five years expect to spend some or all of their capital on holidays, cars and hobbies rather than save up a nest egg for their kids. You.

THE TIME BOMB

The Baby Boomer time bomb is going to blow up in our faces, and we'll be left with the clean-up bill. This is what it comes down to: read it and weep.

1. Loads of Them – not very many of Us

The number of pensioners in the UK is going to engulf the population. Right now, there are 9.8 million pensioners living in the UK. Old age Boomers will soar to 16.1 million by 2032. Meanwhile, the number of people in the UK aged between 16 and 50 will fall by 1.5 million over the next twenty-five years.

2. They're not going away any time soon

Healthier lifestyles and improved medical care are delaying the inevitable like never before. On average men in non-manual jobs can now expect to live to nearly 80 and women until 83.

3. There isn't enough money to go around

By the year 2030, the cost of elderly entitlement programmes will be about double what it is today. There simply won't be enough working adults to cover the national pension and healthcare bill. And they haven't set any money aside to make up the difference. The current deficit for public sector pensions is approaching £1 trillion.

4. Someone's got to pay

There are three options. We could borrow more money (and let our children pick up the bill). We could pay double the tax we do now (and live our adult lives in poverty). Or we could halve our parents' pensions and healthcare (and watch them rot).

Unless we come across an almighty pot of gold, one of these options is going to become reality. Surveys show that affluent Boomers are more interested in spending their money now, rather than saving for their own care. And 20 per cent of them have no private pension and plan to rely entirely on state handouts. But why on earth should we work our fingers to the bone to support people who were too selfish and short-sighted to look out for themselves?

THE FACTS OF LIFE

Graduates are joining the dole queue as soon as they leave university, while their parents retire on cosy nest eggs. First-time buyers are struggling to pay off mortgages on shoe boxes as the older generation buys second homes abroad. Young families are struggling to provide the basics as their grandparents embark on another cruise. Don't allow the love for your parents to get in the way of the facts:

THE FUTURE IS BLEAK

IT'S ALL THEIR FAULT

WE'VE GOT TO DEAL WITH IT RIGHT NOW

The money that we're forced to borrow from the Bank of Mum and Dad is money that they stole from us in the first place. They stole it because the Fred Goodwins of this world have convinced themselves that greed is good; because people like Jeremy Clarkson love themselves more than anyone else; because the millions of men and women like Hazel Blears will only ever act in their own self-interest. They are the most selfish generation ever to have lived.

Nothing can stop the Boomer time bomb going off in 2011. We're saddled with the cost of keeping them, on top of the trillions of pounds of economic debt that they have piled up. But millions of Boomers still have years left before they retire. If we act now, we can prevent them from making things worse.

We can't remove Boomers from the company boardrooms. But we can vote Boomer politicians from office. The general election is our opportunity to kick them out.

06.05.2010
is the day we take control

PLAN OF ACTION

STEP 1.
CHOOSE YOUR CANDIDATE
Log on to www.itsalltheirfault.com.
You'll find a full list of candidates standing in your local area, together with their age and the party they belong to. Choose a candidate under the age of 46. If there isn't a young candidate standing, choose someone aged 65 and over.

STEP 2.
MAIL YOUR CANDIDATE
You'll find a ready-written letter on the website.
Email it to the candidate that you're going to vote for. They need to know why you're giving them your vote, and this will do the job.

STEP 3.
VOTE
Whatever you do on Election Day, make sure you vote.
And make sure you vote non-Boomer.

Imagine, waking up the day after the election with a new generation in power. With enough young people in Parliament, we could force the government to abolish tuition fees, or bring back student grants. We could force them to build affordable homes for us, get tough on City fat cats, or speed up action on the environment. We could even force Boomers to work longer for their pensions. Anything is possible if we are in charge.

There are 24 million people under the age of 46 eligible to vote in the UK. Only 27 million people voted in the last general election. We can make a difference if we all get out and vote.

REMOVE ALL DOUBT

Make no mistake, a vote against Boomers isn't ageist; it's a vote against a single generation. If you can't find a young candidate in your area, you should vote for a pensioner. Having lived through the Depression and/or the last war, pensioners, at the very least, understand the value of prudence and selflessness.

Don't be fooled into thinking that young politicians lack the necessary experience. We couldn't possibly do a worse job than the Baby Boomers. As Chloe Smith, the youngest MP in Parliament says, 'If you're good enough, you're old enough.'

People often say they don't vote because all the major parties seem the same, and they're right: they are. Ever since the Boomers took office in the Eighties the old distinctions of Left and Right have been blurred into policies that benefited only them.

REMEMBER:

it's the Boomer MPs who have presided over the worst global recession in living memory. They set the rules for the banks, they allowed them to take crazy risks, and then used our money to bail the system out.

REMEMBER:

it's the Boomer MPs who were caught red-handed fiddling expenses, stealing public money for castle moats and luxury cars.

REMEMBER:

not a single Boomer politician has paid for their education, or had to borrow six times their salary for a place to live, or had to scrabble for a low-paid short-term job. They can't possibly act in our interest, because they have no idea what it's like to live like us.

Let's be realistic: not every person over the age of 45 is selfish or on the fiddle. But time and again, Baby Boomers have proved that, when they're left in charge, they are incapable of acting beyond their own self-interest. They don't even make amends when they're caught.

The big banks, which we were forced to bail out, have just paid themselves billions in bonuses again. And the MPs' expenses scandal? Most politicians think they've done nothing wrong. 'We're expected to live on rations,' says MP Alan Duncan, the man David Cameron chose to sort out Tory expense claims. 'We're treated like shit,' he says. This is the man who charged the public £4,000 for the upkeep of his lawn.

THE TIME IS NOW

It doesn't matter who you vote for, so the old saying goes, the government always wins. But the government we vote in will be less selfish and greedy if we give ourselves a voice.

We have a responsibility to act; not only to ourselves, but to our own kids. Apathy is no longer an option. Ignoring the problem will only make it worse. We've been left with a £754 billion bill to pay back; the highest national debt for more than thirty years. Our parents won't be paying any of that money off themselves; they'll be retired before we make a down payment on the interest.

The choice is simple. We can sit back and watch the Baby Boomers pour our future down the drain. Or we can take control and make plans for ourselves.

06.05.2010 IS OUR BIG CHANCE

LOG ON TO WWW.ITSALLTHEIRFAULT.COM AND GET READY TO BOOT THEM OUT

The Friday Project
An imprint of HarperCollins*Publishers*
77–85 Fulham Palace Road
Hammersmith, London W6 8JB

www.thefridayproject.co.uk
www.harpercollins.co.uk

First published by The Friday Project in 2010

1

A catalogue record for this book
is available from the British Library

ISBN 978-0-00-737176-1

www.itsalltheirfault.com

www.ingramcontent.com/pod-product-compliance
Ingram Content Group UK Ltd.
Pitfield, Milton Keynes, MK11 3LW, UK
UKHW020843190325
456436UK00004B/10